Dorothea Ernst

30 Minutes

Sustainability

Bibliographic information from the German National Library
The German National Library lists this publication in the German National Bibliography. Detailed bibliographic information can be found online at http://dnb.d-nb.de.

ISBN 978-3-96739-083-4

Cover design: die imprimatur, Hainburg
Cover concept: Martin Zech Design, Bremen
Translation: Dr. Bettina von Stamm, München
Copyediting: Anja Hilgarth, Herzogenaurach
Author portrait: Silvia Schulze
Typesetting: Zerosoft, Timisoara
Printing: Print on demand, Germany

First published under the title '30 Minuten Nachhaltigkeit' in 2020 by GABAL Verlag, Germany

www.linkedin.com/in/dfernst/

Know more in 30 minutes!

This book is designed for you to quickly absorb concise and well-founded information. You will be led through the book with the help of a guidance system, allowing you to capture the essentials within your personal time quota (from 10 to 30 minutes).

Short reading time

You can read the entire book in 30 minutes. If you have less time, you can focus on those sections that contain the most relevant information for you.

- **Key information is printed in grey.**

- Key questions with page references at the beginning of each chapter allow quick orientation: scroll straight to the page that closes your knowledge gap.

- *Numerous summaries within the chapters allow a quick cross-reading.*

- A fast reader at the end of the book summarises all important points.

- An index makes it easy to look up particular terms.

Contents

Preface

Today is a time of great change. Corona has slowed down the world, system-relevant institutions and global dependencies are now visible. This book, which was written before Corona, helps to show how good life for all can be possible in the long term.

What is sustainability? Everyone has experienced that money that is spent today will no longer be available tomorrow; that the bread I eat in the morning can no longer fill me up in the evening. **Good housekeeping is at the core of sustainability.** Sustainable action is moderate and oriented towards the well-being of all, today and tomorrow. But what is 'moderate' for you? What is 'well-being of all'? How long does 'tomorrow' last?

There are diverse answers to these questions, and they are as diverse as the people who provide them. Nevertheless, there are some anchor points that humanity has agreed upon. The 17 Sustainable Development Goals (SDGs) of the United Nations were drawn up through a long international negotiation process. They were published in 2015, to be achieved by 2030.

The Agenda 2030 goals provide politicians, companies and civil society with a common framework for action.

But how to implement these goals in companies? Can a company be profitable and contribute to the sustainable development of humanity at the same time? Is this the role of business, the task of companies at all?

The answer is: yes! Because no other form of organisation brings new ideas into the world faster and more efficiently than a company. Business is the greatest engine of change. And it is already happening. More and more companies are consciously working on the implementation of the UN Sustainable Development Goals. In this book you will learn:

- what is meant by sustainable development,
- about the role the United Nations 2030 Agenda plays on the path to sustainable development,
- how disruptive technologies could support this transformation,
- how you can contribute to sustainable development by walking the twin path of personal development and professional effectiveness.

I have been on this journey for more than 20 years. Discover with me how exciting and rewarding it is.

Dr. Dorothea Ernst

30 MINUTES

1. The state of the world

Every day we are bombarded with a wide range of information about the **precarious state of the world**: The impact of Corona, climate change, plastic waste in the ocean, refugees and wars are just some of the problems we face. At the same time, new technologies, such as digitisation, robotics, biotechnology and neuroscience, lead to **disruptive changes in our work and personal lives.** They offer tremendous innovation potential, but the speed of their development can be deeply unsettling.

The more we know, the less we can predict, this is the knowledge paradox we experience. How can I find my way in a time when knowledge is increasing daily? A look at history helps. It helps us to recognise that humanity has an almost inexhaustible level of crowd creativity. Humanity can create amazing changes as soon as common goals are agreed and we align behind the same story, the same narrative.

1.1 Where we come from

For a long time, people struggled with three main problems: **hunger, war and disease**. Over the millennia, a variety of technologies and organisational forms have been developed to deal with these challenges. But only recently **new challenges** have been added to the scourges of humanity.

UN Millennium Development Goals

1. Eradicate extreme poverty and hunger
2. Achieve universal primary education for all
3. Promote gender equality and empower women
4. Reduce child mortality
5. Improve maternal health
6. Combat HIV/AIDS, malaria and other diseases
7. Ensure environmental sustainability
8. Develop a global partnership for development

Obesity and hunger

Hunger has not been fully eradicated, but one of the successes of the UN Millennium Goals is that hunger in the world has been reduced by 50% since the year 2000. Did you know that today more people worldwide suffer from obesity than from hunger?

Victims of civilization and war

Every year more people die in car accidents than in war. There are still wars, but their nature has changed.

In the past, power and wealth were linked to the possession of material goods such as land and raw materials. In today's knowledge society, power and wealth are associated with access to non-material goods such as attention, knowledge, data and energy. This led to new ways of warfare such as cyber war and new sources of criminal exploitation such as data theft.
Individual aggression today also shows in different ways: Did you know that the suicide rate among young people in the UK has almost doubled over the past decade due to bullying on social media?

Health care and sickness

Average life expectancy has doubled from around 40 to more than 80 years over the last century. Well-known and practiced hygiene and the development of health systems are the main reasons for this development. But in the same period, new viruses have been brought in from the animal kingdom and biological anomalies habe been detected creating new risks for humanity. In addition, our fast-paced and hectic modern world is leading to an increase in mental health issues such as depression and ADHD. Many suffer from loneliness or a feeling of insignificance.

Technology is changing the world

The main reasons for the impressive progress of Western societies is the triumph of technology and the associated changes in the way humanity organises itself. The economist Nikolai Kondratjev published his obser-

vations of the **long waves of the economy** in a Berlin magazine in 1926.
One of the hallmarks of these Kondratjev cycles is that readily available resources and skills that have found little or no attention so far now enter the general consciousness and suddenly acquire wider significance. They mark boosts of innovation, triggered by certain inventions, which keep changing the whole of society until their innovation potential is exhausted. Alongside the transition to the next cycle, there is always a profound change in society. The **Kondratjev cycles are therefore also processes of social reorganisation.** Since the beginning of industrialisation there have been five such long waves or cycles, each triggered by groundbreaking inventions or the spread of so-called basic innovations. A sixth wave is already emerging.

1st wave: steam engine, cotton, textile industry
The first wave was triggered by the invention and use of steam engines and marks the beginning of the first industrial revolution and early mechanisation – in Germany around 1780 to 1842 and in England around 1760.

2nd wave: steelmaking, railway, steamship, telegraphy
The second wave began about 60 years later, taking place between 1843 and 1894 during the so-called 'Gründerzeit'. The technology drivers here were steam shipping and the invention of the Briton Henry Besse-

mer which made it possible to mass-produce steel. This was an important requirement for the construction of railway lines. In addition, the mining industry expanded in this wave, and telegraphy was invented.

3rd wave: electrical engineering, power generation, chemistry

The third long wave of world economy from 1895 to the end of the 1930s was shaped in particular by technical innovations such as electrification, heavy machinery, the internal combustion engine and with it the beginning of the age of the automobile. The invention of the light bulb and the development of basic technologies in electrical engineering and chemistry also happened during this period.

4th wave: petrochemicals, individual mobility, computers

The fourth Kondratjev wave was particularly characterised by the automotive, aerospace and plastics industries. Its basic innovations were the integrated circuit, the transistor, the first computers, nuclear energy and the aircraft. It lasted from 1940 to around 1990.

5th wave: biotechnology and digitisation

Since 1990 we have been experiencing the fifth wave, its core innovations being information and communication technologies as well as biotechnology. Globalisation is another key feature of this wave.

6th wave: **psychosocial health, neuroscience, sustainability**

Since around 2010 we have been experiencing the emergence of a sixth Kondratjev wave. This one is shaped by the topics of health, wellness, education and sustainability. This makes the healthcare market an important key market for economic development.

World population growth

At the beginning of this chapter I highlighted that humans are extraordinarily creative and capable of change. One result of this is the remarkable population growth that started with the industrial revolution. At the beginning of the 19th century only one billion people were living on our planet, and it took them 123 years to double. But they only needed eleven years, from 1999 to 2011, to grow from six to seven billion. For the year 2050 statisticians of the United Nations forecast a world population of approx. ten billion people, for 2100 approx. eleven billion. After that, no further population growth is expected.

30 *Looking at the history of industrialisation since the end of the 18th century, one can rightly speak of a success story for mankind: improvements in life expectancy, standard of living, the general level of education and much more. However, this progress has a price that is becoming apparent today.*

1.2 The world today

Every day we hear and read about the multitude of global and national challenges. By contrast, we generally learn little about the causes of these challenges. In its 2006 Living Planet Report, the World Wide Fund for Nature (WWF) published its first graphic that illustrates the unsustainability of our growth logic in just one picture. This graph is updated on a regular basis. Its essence, however, hasn't changed much over recent years.

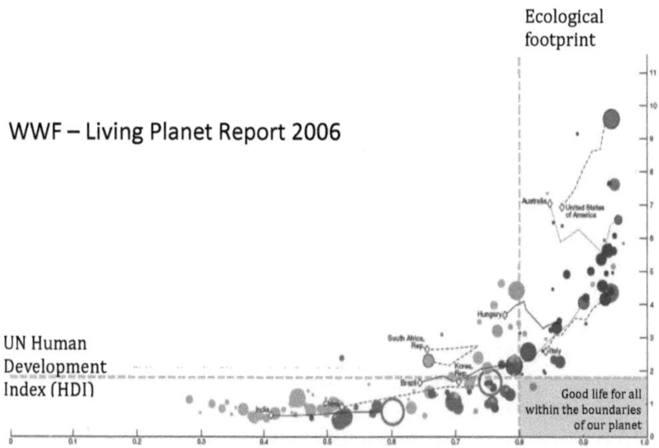

Fig. 1: Unsustainable logic of progress

The horizontal axis of the graph represents the **Human Development Index (HDI)**, the vertical axis the **Ecological Footprint.** Sustainability would be achieved if everyone lived at a high HDI level without destroying ecological resources. In the graphic, this would mean being in the grey rectangle at the bottom right. All countries are represented by a circle. The size of the circle corresponds with the size of the population. The two largest circles represent India (left) and China (right) with more than one billion inhabitants.

Today the industrialised nations (Europe, North America, Australia and some Asian countries) offer their citizens a life with a high HDI, but at the expense of excessive resource consumption. The so-called developing countries in Africa and Asia do indeed operate within the planetary boundaries, but do not offer the majority of their citizens good living conditions.

HDI – a measure of progress
The Human Development Index (HDI) is a measure used by the UN to describe a country's level of development. It not only takes into account the gross domestic product (GDP) per capita, but also the average life expectancy as a measure of health and the level of education of the citizens. The HDI is normalised to the number 1. All people in the world should have the opportunity to achieve a high level of development, that is, to live with an HDI of 0.8 or more.

Ecological footprint – a measure of resource consumption
Mathis Wackernagel and William Rees came up with the concept of the ecological footprint in the early 1990s. It allows to account for ecological resources, comparable to financial accounting in business. The ecological footprint measures the consumption of natural resources in

global hectares (gha) per person and year. In this way, it records people's resource consumption. Among other things, it takes energy, food, clothing, waste disposal and carbon sequestration into consideration. It also records how much nature (= ecological capital) is (still) available to the people in that country.

There are two important reasons for the imbalance: the **massive population growth** since the beginning of the 20th century and the global **economic system, which is geared towards maximising consumption and profit**, including its linear value chains and the steadily increasing consumption of resources despite increases in efficiency. The curved arrow in the following graphic illustrates the dynamic of this development:

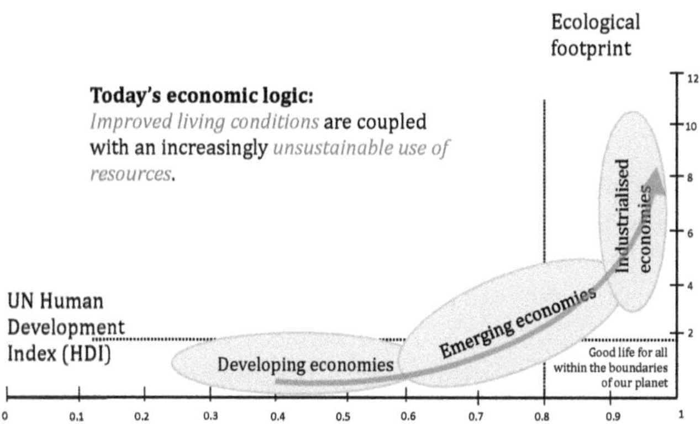

Fig. 2: Problematic development dynamics

Many are calling for the great transformation

Ever since the Fridays for Future movement came into being, the public has become increasingly aware that **radical changes are necessary** in order to enable a good long-term life for everyone on our planet.

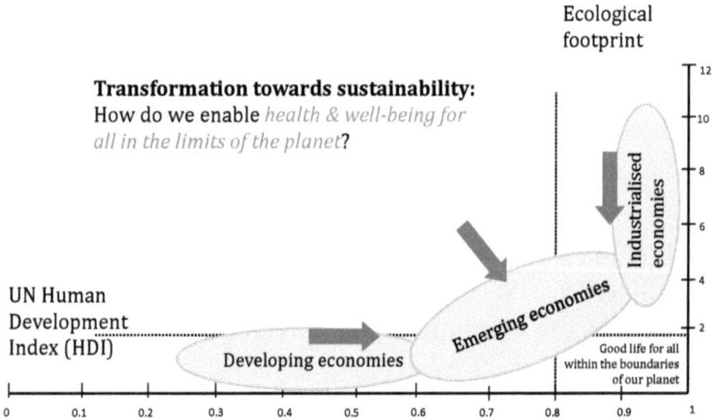

Fig. 3: Necessary changes

However, there is no standard solution that is right for everyone:

- The **industrialised economies** must find ways to reduce their resource consumption while ensuring that their citizens can maintain their high standard of living.
- When building their economies, infrastructures and social systems, the **emerging countries'** economies should pay attention to sustainability right from the start.

- **Developing countries** must ensure that the living conditions of their citizens are improved without significantly increasing their ecological footprint.

The United Nations uses the Human Development Index to measure the social dimension of sustainability. The ecological footprint is used to record the environmental aspects of sustainability. The WWF has summarised the state of the world with these two parameters in one graph. To achieve sustainability a global systems change is necessary.

1.3 Systems transformation ahead

The term **systems transformation** has become an indispensable part of today's public discussion. But what is a **system**? What is meant by **transformation** in this context?

The term system

A system is a whole made up of several individual parts. It is a definable, natural or artificial 'structure', which consists of different components that are (can be) considered as a collective whole, due to certain ordered relationships with each other. The two main categories are:

Natural systems

The natural systems are real systems that have arisen **without any specific human influence** and that are self-sustaining, e.g.

- quantum system, atoms, molecules, planetary system (described by physics and chemistry)
- living or organic systems such as cells, organs, nervous system, psyche, ecosystems (described by biology, medicine, psychology)

Artificial systems

The artificial systems were **conceived and constructed by humans.** They can be material or immaterial in nature, but do, however, often combine both. Examples are:

- technical systems, e.g. tools, machines, computers
- economic systems, e.g. currencies, stocks, insurance policies
- social systems, e.g. family, ethnicity, association, religious community, company, organisation
- socio-technical systems, e.g. information system, internet, railway network, electricity infrastructure
- socio-economic systems, e.g. health system, pension system, economic system including tax law and international trade agreements

Systems transformation

The Kondratjev waves, already described in Section 1.1, are each accompanied by far-reaching social changes.

You can imagine it like this: over a long period of time for humans (several decades), a cultural behaviour has developed, for example the use of horse-drawn carriages to cover greater distances. This solution to the mobility problem is known to everyone and is underpinned by social rules. Alternative solutions are seen as crazy. We experience times of unconsciously **dominant culture**.

But unobserved by the public, pioneers develop new solutions to existing problems, such as the use of automobiles at the end of the 19th century. For a long time, these were relatively unknown and not really accepted, often met with scepticism or resistance. But they contain the essential characteristics of a new, **emergent culture**. The new solution, and with it the new cultural behaviour, only begins to establish itself when it can solve old problems much better than the known means, or when new problems arise that can only be solved by the new concept. Using the automobile example, they take up less space than horses and carriages, are more flexible and allow individual transport for everyone.

As soon as the new solution starts to spread, a phase of **disruptive innovation** arises. This time is characterised by a cultural struggle between the old and the new. For some time, both systems exist in parallel. People are experiencing a time of great dynamism and uncertainty. They are faced with the question of when is the right time to switch to the new system. The **systems**

transformation is complete as soon as the new culture has spread so widely that it has become dominant.

Today: double systems transformation

We are currently in a very special situation, in as much as two systems changes are happening almost at the same time. The sixth Kondratjev wave follows the fifth with a delay of only about ten years. In simple terms, we have been in the disruption phase of the systems change from **analogue to digital** for around ten years. The trigger for the change was probably the introduction of the iPhone in 2008. The smartphone has radically changed the way we communicate and deal with data in the industrial context. New cultural skills, such as the use of apps or the implementation of Bill Gates' vision 'Information: always and everywhere', were initially developed by pioneers and young people and are currently being learned by the entire population.

At the end of 2015, the second systems transformation was heralded by the Paris Agreement and the publication of the UN Sustainable Development Goals. It refers to the transformation of our global economic system from **profit orientation to sustainable value creation.** Until recently, we have operated under the premises of maximising productivity and optimising profits. This was based on economic theories and their basic assumptions, which had not been questioned and corrected for more than 100 years. As a consequence, the growth myth is still postulated. This also means that it is accepted that many effects of economic activity are borne by the general public as so-called externalities (e.g. the costs for the final storage of radioactive waste).

If we want to achieve the goal that in 2050 all people lead a good life within the boundaries of our planet, it will be necessary to follow a new economic logic. This should be geared towards generating corporate profits while simultaneously creating ecological and social benefits.

We live in times of double systems transformation: 30

- ***Digitisation is bringing about major changes in the way we communicate and how businesses, cities and communities deal with data and information. We all learn new cultural skills.***
- ***Parallel to the upheavals in digitisation, the transformation of our global economic system is increasingly visible – coupled with the term sustainability. Essentially, it is about changing our concept of economic success. In future, this will no longer be measured only in terms of profitability, but also in terms of the creation of social and ecological benefits.***

30 MINUTES

Since when has the concept of 'sustainability' been around?
Page 26

What contribution is the UN making to sustainable development in the world?
Page 28

How can the change towards sustainable development be initiated?
Page 32

2. Sustainable development

Aristotle (384–322 BC) presented the first systematic economic theory. He proclaimed it to be important to operate in the 'house' ('oĩkos') according to clear, natural 'laws' ('nómos'). In the middle of the 13th century Thomas Aquinas wrote the doctrine of the 'just price' in his work *Summa Theologica*. He classified agriculture and handicrafts as more important than trade. He also pointed out that the pursuit of profit must not harm the weaker or the general public.

It wasn't until the middle of the 18th century that economics became a science. According to Wikipedia: '**Economy is the totality of all facilities and actions that serve the planned satisfaction of needs**'. This modern definition summarises a very complex network of concrete and highly abstract activities. Economic activity takes place around the world every day and has a profound effect on all of our lives. But are people's needs actually being met today? What exactly are our needs?

2.1 The roots of sustainability

The principle of sustainability was first formulated in writing by **Hans Carl von Carlowitz in 1713**. He founded the discipline of forestry. He wrote his book *Sylvicultura Oeconomica, oder haußwirthliche Nachricht und Naturmäßige Anweisung zur Wilden Baum-Zucht*, in a time of an energy crisis. The ore mines and smelters in the German Ore Mountains used a lot of wood. Population and urban growth intensified the 'wood shortage'. Regulated forestry as well as laws, ecological standards or certifications for afforestation did not exist. He therefore demanded that nature and its raw materials be treated with respect and 'care'. He criticised the overexploitation of the forests designed to generate short-term profits.

Two and a half centuries later, in **1972, the Club of Rome published its 'Limits to Growth'**. Its central message was: '*If the current increase in world population, industrialisation, environmental pollution, food production and the exploitation of natural resources continues unchanged, the absolute limits of growth on earth will be reached in the course of the next hundred years.*' (Meadows, 1972)

The post-war economic miracle brought prosperity to the western world. The developing countries, however, have not been able to keep up with the progress of the market economies. In order to counter this social imbalance, and the associated potential for conflict and war, the United Nations (UN) became active in the mid-1980s. The so-called **Brundtland Commission** published the report **Our Common Future in 1987**. In this report, the term '**sustainable development**' was coined in its current meaning. These are the two best-known definitions:

- *'Sustainable development is development that meets the needs of the present without compromising the ability of future generations to meet their own needs'.* (Brundtland Report, p. 41) (Focus: intergenerational equity)
- *'In essence, sustainable development is a process of change in which the exploitation of resources, the direction of investments, the orientation of technological development; and institutional change are all in harmony and enhance both current and future potential to meet human needs and aspirations'.* (Brundtland Report, p. 43) (Focus: holistic behaviour change)

The term sustainability comes from the field of forestry. The concept of 'sustainable development' was coined in 1987 as part of the global poverty and environmental debate. Both ideas share the concern for a healthy, moderate use of natural resources. This is seen as a prerequisite for people to be able to lead a good life today and in the future.

2.2 The UN Sustainable Development Goals (SDGs)

The United Nations (UN) has its roots in The Hague Peace Conferences and in the League of Nations. Already after the First World War the League had the goal of permanently securing world peace. In 1945, shortly after the end of the Second World War, 51 founding members signed the United Nations Charter, which is also known as the UN Constitution. In essence, since its foundation the UN has pursued the following five goals:

- maintaining **international peace** and security,
- protecting **human rights**,
- delivering **humanitarian aid**,
- promoting **sustainable development** and
- upholding **international law**.

Today the UN has 193 members. Both German states did not join the UN until 1973. A large number of UN organisations around the world are working on the implementation of the goals.

Common goals: a well-kept secret

Interestingly, most of us are not aware of either the Millennium Goals or the current Sustainable Development Goals. It is also little known that the Millennium Development Goals have essentially been achieved, which was by no means foreseeable when they were published in 2000. It is therefore not surprising that the 17

UN **Sustainable Development Goals (SDGs) published in 2015** are also a well-kept secret for many. They were formulated in political language and legislative logic. It takes additional effort to translate the goals into corporate language. This work is currently being done by many organisations.

The UN Sustainable Development Goals	
Goal 1	End poverty in all its forms everywhere
Goal 2	End hunger, achieve food security and improved nutrition, and promote sustainable agriculture
Goal 3	Ensure healthy lives and promote well-being for all at all ages
Goal 4	Ensure inclusive and equitable quality education and promote lifelong learning opportunities for all
Goal 5	Achieve gender equality and empower all women and girls
Goal 6	Ensure availability and sustainable management of water and sanitation for all
Goal 7	Ensure access to affordable, reliable, sustainable and modern energy for all
Goal 8	Promote sustained, inclusive and sustainable economic growth, full and productive employment and decent work for all
Goal 9	Build resilient infrastructure, promote inclusive and sustainable industrialisation, and foster innovation
Goal 10	Reduce income inequality within and among countries
Goal 11	Make cities and human settlements inclusive, safe, resilient and sustainable

Goal 12	Ensure sustainable consumption and production patterns
Goal 13	Take urgent action to combat climate change and its impacts by regulating emissions and promoting developments in renewable energy
Goal 14	Conserve and sustainably use the oceans, seas and marine resources for sustainable development
Goal 15	Protect, restore and promote sustainable use of terrestrial ecosystems, sustainably manage forests, combat desertification, and halt and reverse land degradation and halt biodiversity loss
Goal 16	Promote peaceful and inclusive societies for sustainable development, provide access to justice for all and build effective, accountable and inclusive institutions at all levels
Goal 17	Strengthen the means of implementation and revitalise the Global Partnership for Sustainable Development

Fig. 4: UN Sustainable Development Goals – SDGs

With the implementation of the UN Sustainable Development Goals (SDGs), mankind will not have achieved the transformation to sustainability nor the goal that all people live well within the planetary boundaries. They are to be understood as a milestone in a longer development journey. The SDGs give us a medium-term orientation on the path that we must find together to achieve the long-term goal of a good life for all within the planetary boundaries.

It is obvious that no social group, no nation alone can achieve these goals. Therefore, everyone is called to work on them. Sub-goals are defined for each of these goals, 169 in total. Since 2016, most countries around the world have been working on translating the goals and sub-goals into concrete measures and finding appropriate indicators to monitor their implementation. All measures should make sense in their geographical and cultural context. Therefore, there is no standardised approach to implementation, but plenty of room for creativity, creative drive and innovation.

30

The 17 UN Sustainable Development Goals form the agenda for the peaceful and sustainable development of mankind jointly defined by the 193 states of the United Nations. They are to be achieved by 2030 and are a milestone on the pathway to a good life for all within the planetary boundaries.

2.3 A change in direction through backcasting

There are two fundamentally different approaches to planning the activities of companies and other organisations: forecasting and backcasting.

Forecasting – planning with historical data

Behind forecasting is a process where future developments are forecast on the basis of historical and current data as well as the analysis of trends. Typical areas of application are, for example, production planning, planning of sales figures, resource planning, logistics planning, e.g. transport requirements and cost optimisation processes.

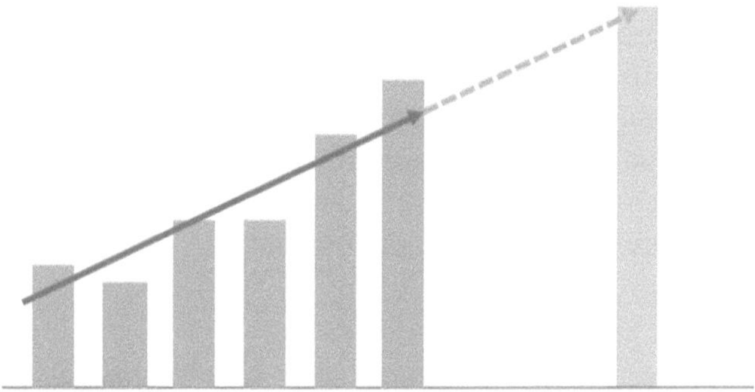

Fig. 5: Forecasting approach

A distinction is made between **qualitative methods**, such as the Delphi method or market analysis, and

quantitative methods, such as averaging, drift methods or time series approaches. Nowadays, learning algorithms and artificial intelligence are used in forecasting processes.

Forecasting never delivers absolutely reliable statements about the future, it is fraught with risks. Good forecasting therefore always indicates the degree of uncertainty that has to be expected. The quality of a forecast always depends on the quality and timeliness of the data used.

Forecasting is a good planning method in stable market situations with an existing customer base. In addition, it works well for so-called **incremental innovations**, minor product changes that can be developed in standardised innovation processes.

Backcasting – planning with a vision for the future

If, however, you find yourself in highly dynamic, complex markets, you want to open a new market or design a strategic change in direction, backcasting is the planning method of choice. The starting point for backcasting is not the historical development, but a defined desired end state, described in a vision. In order to implement this vision, a change of course is usually necessary, or a **radical** or **disruptive innovation**.

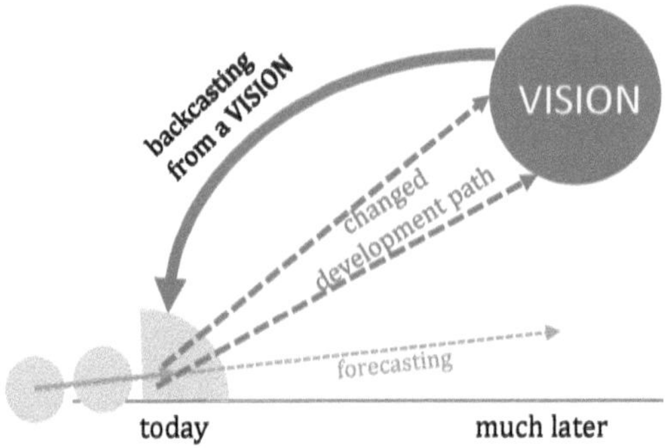

Fig. 6: Procedure for backcasting

A backcasting process usually consists of six steps:

1. Problem definition

A **problem definition** should always be included at the beginning of a backcasting process. It is important to identify and involve all those affected, which can sometimes be difficult and tedious. In this process step, mediation can be helpful as a method for identifying topics. It is important that all voices are heard and taken into account and that the problem with all its facets is described **systemically**.

2. Co-creation of a vision

After the problem has been described from different perspectives, the **vision formation** also takes place with the involvement of all those affected. A vision sums up the big, common goal of all in one easy-to-communicate sentence. This sentence must be comprehensible both rationally and emotionally. The best-known example is the vision that J. F. Kennedy formulated before the United States Congress on May 25, 1961: '*I believe this nation should have achieved its goal of having a man land on the moon and bring him back safely by the end of the decade* [the 1960s].'

At the end of the vision development process it is helpful to translate the vision into **strategic goals** for the various stakeholders. If possible, progress indicators should be assigned to the goals at this stage. These indicators help to make a meaningful inventory – directed at achieving the vision. Based on the vision, the associated strategic goals and indicators a **desired state** is defined. (Sometimes this activity is also seen as the first step in determining the initial situation and is developed in the next phase of the process.)

3. Determining the status quo

As soon as the vision and the strategic goals associated with its achievement are clear, the determination of the current situation begins. It is very important to pay attention to reliable data. The GIGO principle applies ('garbage in – garbage out'). The **current state** is typically determined through interviews with the problem owners and the evaluation of (publicly) available statistics, research reports, market analysis, etc. Now is the time to set up an ongoing project team and add experts to it.

The planning task arises from the gap between the desired future and the current state. The innovation task now is to identify and design solutions that enable this gap to be bridged.

4. Ideation – finding solutions

Classic idea generation processes can be carried out to identify possible solutions. These are usually divided into three steps:

- **Generation of ideas**: It's about quantity, that is, the quick collection of many ideas. Methods such as brainstorming, brainwriting or lateral thinking are used here. In this process step, idea seeds are developed that usually only affect one aspect of the problem.
- **Idea development**: It's about quality, that is, the further development of idea seeds into ideas that take into account many aspects of the problem. In addition, methods such as De Bono's six thinking hats or specifically developed idea development frameworks are used.
- **Clustering**: In this process step, many similar ideas are bundled around a topic or structured in terms of time in a roadmap.

It is important to conduct this creative process with the involvement of all stakeholders and some who are unfamiliar with the problem. Due to their impartiality, the latter bring in 'disruptive' or 'crazy' ideas that are usually not seen by those affected. There are now well-tested software platforms that support this process. This way people from many countries and many different organisations can come together to jointly develop solution pathways.

5. Prioritisation and planning

At the end of the ideation phase, there are usually more ideas than resources to implement them. Therefore, prioritisation is necessary. Two types of prioritisation criteria can be distinguished: **feasibility** and **effectiveness.**

Feasibility means realisability, that is, a solution is in line with scientific knowledge as well as legal, economic or other framework conditions. Feasibility is usually expressed in the context of prioritisation in qualitative metrics, for example 'simple – complicated – complex', 'short-term – medium-term – long-term', 'use of resources: low – medium – high'.

Effectiveness describes the ability or property to produce a desired effect. To assess the effectiveness of a solution criteria such as the following can be helpful: 'useful – necessary – obstacle on a critical path', 'step towards vision: small – medium – large', 'depth of change: small (but quickly feasible intermediate step that buys time) – large (would lead directly to the desired end result, but is very resource-intensive)'.

It is helpful to visualise the results of the prioritisation using a **pathway map**. Similar to roadmaps that have been used frequently since the early 2000s, a pathway map is used to visualise a strategy or a project plan. It differs from a roadmap in that it not only depicts an industry, but also describes change at the systems level. The first pathway map was presented in 2010 by the World Business Council for Sustainable Development to visualise VISION 2050.

6. Adaptive or agile implementation

Project teams are set up and begin their work. During the implementation, one cannot learn from past experiences. It is therefore advisable to regularly update the original starting point. As in agile software development, changes lead to adjustments in the next steps. In other words: The implementation work is designed to be agile and adaptive, **in small, conscious steps, with the big, common goal in mind.**

The Natural Step (TNS)

In 1989 Karl-Henrik Robèrt founded the NGO The Natural Step (TNS). After the Brundtland Report was published in 1987, Robert developed the TNS framework. He defined four system conditions for the sustainability of human activity on earth: three ecological and one socio-economic. The Natural Step also pioneered backcasting with the four system conditions, which are also known as sustainability principles.

30

Since the implementation of the UN Sustainable Development Goals can be understood as an intermediate step in the profound transformation of our global economic system, backcasting is a useful planning method. In a six-step process, starting with the problem definition, a vision is formulated by all affected stakeholders. Then the current state is determined relating to the jointly desired future. Ideas to achieve the vision are developed, prioritised and implemented with optimal use of the available resources. The work is agile, i.e. reacting flexibly to changing framework conditions. New knowledge and experiences are continuously noticed and used.

30 MINUTES

3. Sustainable business

Until recently, growth was the unquestioned creed of the economy. Entrepreneurial and economic thinking and acting were geared towards optimising profits and gross domestic product. In return, unintentional negative side effects with regard to ecology or social justice were accepted over and over again. The transition to sustainable development changes this behaviour.

3.1 Sustainable day-to-day business

The day-to-day, or operational, business includes all corporate activities that are directly related to the achievement of the company's purpose. It occurs in various corporate functions or departments, based on the principle of the division of labour, e.g. accounting and controlling, marketing, sales, customer service, purchasing, production, IT administration, human resources and corporate communication. Most companies follow standardised operating processes in order to act efficiently and conserve resources. What has to change in order to make day-to-day business not only financially sustainable, but also bring them in line with the Brundtland Report and the SDGs?

Success metric

The aim of companies is to serve the needs of their customers with the goods and services offered and thus to make a profit. So far, the success of a company has essentially been based on its profitability. This is about to change. Many well-known management consultancies published studies a few years ago in which they show how companies can contribute to **good growth** in the future. Good growth differs from bad in that

- **Economic, ecological and social value creation** takes place at the same time,
- Externalities are priced in (e.g. CO_2 tax),

- It is taken into account that many **natural resources** (e.g. topsoil, phosphorus and nitrogen cycle) are scarce and **absolutely irreplaceable**.

Sales and customer support

Sales and customer care are classically geared towards sensing the implicit needs, i.e. the needs that the customer is not yet aware of, and doing everything to ensure the greatest possible customer satisfaction. The natural counterpart for sales is operational purchasing. The natural interlocutors for customer care are those who use the products in their day-to-day work. In many companies, the issue of sustainability does not yet play a conscious role in these environments. The following questions can help to deepen the customer relationship even further:

- **How do we support our customers today in making their contribution to the implementation of the SDGs?**
- How can we support our customers in developing into a sustainable company or work with them to implement the SDGs?

Some companies are already consciously looking for suppliers who act carefully and sustainably. In order to be recognisable for them, the following questions should be answered:

- Do we want or can we differentiate ourselves through sustainability?
- If so: how and why?

Purchasing

Purchasing has a major impact on supplying the company with all the materials and services necessary to create value. Cost management is a key issue. If sustainability is taken seriously, however, when choosing a supplier next to cost optimisation **ecological and social criteria** must also be taken into account. New questions for purchasing are:

- Are we opting for the more sustainable alternative, e.g. green electricity, recycled paper?
- How sustainable are our suppliers?
- Could we evolve together?
- Are we ready to break up with suppliers who do not act sustainably?

(Digital) infrastructure

Direct influence is available to many companies when it comes to designing their own infrastructure: this could be through their type of power supply, their buildings or their vehicle fleet, many levers of change are available. IT infrastructure design also holds great potential for sustainable action. **Green IT** deals explicitly with CO_2 optimisation. It is about low energy consumption, modular concepts, possibly outsourcing computing capacity to larger, more scalable data centres. In addition, one can critically question how frequently computers are modernised, and which software is chosen as the company standard. The way in which the IT infrastructure is maintained, new software introduced and how user questions are responded to has a major impact on the well-being and further development of employees, thus on SDG 3 and SDG 4.

Employee well-being

Employees who feel at ease are known to be a key success factor for companies. Therefore, it makes sense to **focus on the well-being of the employees**. In the future, it will no longer be sufficient to implement the legal requirements. Some practical examples of activities that promote employee well-being are:

- Opportunity to get a flu or COVID 19 vaccination and a medical check-up through the company
- Sports activities, activity breaks
- E-bike leasing
- Provision of height-adjustable desks where appropriate
- Further education and training opportunities including personal development
- Organic and vegetarian catering options
- Working time concepts that enable work-life balance

Communication

Do good things and talk about it! This motto can only be implemented if there is good transparency about business activities and their effects. Often companies are not aware of the consequences of their actions. The annual report gives an overview of a company's key financial figures but does not always report on ecological or social contributions. More and more companies are publishing **sustainability reports** for this purpose. This is now a requirement for large corporations. Sustainability is also playing an increasingly important role in companies' digital presence and marketing communications. **Greenwashing**, i.e. pure marketing or PR activities that are not based on legitimate sustainable or socially responsible activity, should be categorically avoided.

Internal communication with an **authentic lived feedback-culture** plays a very important role. It should be made clear to employees that sustainability in the company is not limited to printing less or replacing flights with rail travel or video conferences, but rather that the greatest lever is usually to support customers in being more sustainable through the company's products or services.

30 *There are many ways to make day-to-day business more sustainable. Sustainable supply chains, green IT, feedback culture, etc. are hot topics. In order to implement this, the various functions have to deal with new issues, but this, however, also entails conflicting goals and dilemmas.*

3.2 Sustainable innovation

'Innovation' is derived from the Latin verb 'innovare' ('to renew'). For a long time the term was closely linked to the type of progress associated with the spread of the Kondratjev base-technologies (technology-driven innovation). The **concept of innovation has been expanding** since the beginning of the millennium. Nowadays, for example, it also includes changes in purchasing relationships, corporate communications, business models and general lifestyle. The change to a more sustainable economy calls for a diverse range of innovations.

Business model

A business model describes the way a company generates profits. It helps to **understand, analyse and communicate the key factors of success or failure.** If the success metric changes, as described in the last chapter, the business model will also change. This is a very profound innovation as it typically affects all company processes and functions. It has to be communicated very sensitively and requires a well-orchestrated change process in which all employees are involved, if possible, from the beginning. Companies must always be financially sustainable, i.e. profitable. However, **sustainable business models** do not only maximise financial success, but optimise multiple benefits, e.g. **customer benefits as well as ecological and social ben-**

efits, within the boundaries of healthy profitability. The maximisation task becomes a multidimensional optimisation task. For some time now, there have been types of companies that have overtly integrated sustainability into their corporate purpose, e.g. B. B-Corps (Benefit Corporations), non-profit GmbHs or companies that organise themselves according to the principles of the common good economy such as not for profit Community Interest Companies (C.I.C.s).

New skills

In order to handle this **multidimensional optimisation task** a company needs new skill sets. Some of these exist already, others have to be pioneered and tested by pioneers. More will probably be necessary in the next few years. The following are already being discussed:

Systemic problem definition

A systemic problem definition requires the involvement of all those affected and the agreement on a manageable project scope. Among other things, the following questions need to be clarified:

- What is the scope of the problem under consideration? If it is too narrowly defined, important influencing factors are neglected. Too wide a scope and it could easily lead to overwhelming complexity.
- Which participants are affected, decision-makers, problem solvers, moderators, mediators, transla-

tors? What roles do we need so that the process can be well designed?

- Which communication problems can arise due to different professional experiences (multidisciplinary), belonging to different industries or social groups (multi-stakeholder), belonging to different national cultural backgrounds (multinational)?
- Are there research projects in which we can and should participate?
- Which trends and developments, that have received too little attention so far, should we observe in future?

In the context of innovation management, **systemically defining the problem should be deliberately designed as a separate step** at the beginning of the innovation process. It needs a clearly defined budget that includes travel, resources and moderation costs. This is increasingly made possible by appropriate public funding. In principle, the methods of **design thinking** can be used here as long as society and the environment are taken into account as additional 'customers'.

Innovation criteria for sustainable innovation

Innovation criteria for sustainable innovation can supplement existing criteria. Many companies have **checklists** that are used in product development. These can be expanded to include **ecological** and **social parameters** with relatively little effort. In this context, it is also important to make it clear what will be stopped going forward. A prominent example of this is the use of a red list for certain highly toxic chemical substances.

Multidimensional accounting

Multidimensional accounting and controlling are the basis for holistic or systemic measurement of success. For this purpose, the double-entry bookkeeping, which is currently one-dimensionally fixed on financial key figures, i.e. monetised double-entry bookkeeping, must be expanded to include ecological and social or socially relevant parameters.

Key figures usually go through the following evolution: qualitative -> quantitative -> monetised. Whether a key figure should be monetised and, if so, how this is done, is a very lengthy social coordination process. With this, often many ethical questions have to be clarified, e.g. the value of topsoil, the value of CO_2 not emitted, the value of trust.

Measurement and monitoring

If there is agreement on useful key figures, the next problem arises: How are they measured and which control mechanisms can be established? The focus here is on monitoring and measuring **sustainability-relevant key indicators.**

Tolerance of ambiguity

Tolerance of ambiguity, also known as uncertainty or uncertainty tolerance, is the ability to endure **contradicting** actions and to deal with **ambiguous** situations. Even today, managers have the task to deal with information that seems difficult to understand or even unacceptable, without reacting aggressively or in an undifferentiated way. They have to deal calmly with **dilemmas** and **paradoxes**, and be able to design decision-making processes that allow a good balance.

Partnering

The difference between a partnership and partnering lies in the quality of the cooperation. This can be compared to the difference between a friendship and a marriage or cohabitation. Partnering is about creating a very trusting, long-term business relationship. Then core of this business relationship is the common goal that would not be possible for either partner to achieve in isolation. The **principle applies: 1 + 1> 2.** All partnering parties benefit from the cooperation. **It is a win-win situation.** To do this, they openly share risks and rewards. In the partnering relationship, each party contributes its strengths and, in accordance with clear agreements, other resources and financial means. Roles and responsibilities are clearly defined and continuously reflected on during the process.

Pioneering

The transformation to a sustainable economic system is a process unknown to all of us. There is no silver bullet that promises success. **Together we have to set out and discover new territory.** This is often done with methods and tools that were developed to optimise what is known.

The good thing is that we are all in the same boat. The unfortunate thing is that we are involved in an everyday life which demands more and more results in a seemingly shorter and shorter period of time. Where is the time to breathe and understand what to do?

'Good managers efficiently produce goods, bring them to their customers and close factories,' a top manager told me a few years ago. Success and results in the 'old world' depend on the efficiency, optimisation and control of existing processes and procedures. Efficiently manufactured products are brought from the production facility to the customer by means of optimised logistics via well-developed transport routes – motorways, rail networks, shipping.

But: **sustainable innovation turns everything known on its head.** The task is to develop the courage to break new ground. Metaphorically speaking, this means shifting from the truck on the motorway to cutting a new pathway through a jungle. There is no map and danger could lurk at every turn. Survival depends on a pioneering spirit, adaptability and trust.

Servant leadership

According to a study published in 2015, service leadership leads to very high employee satisfaction. It is particularly helpful in times of great change and uncertainty, in order to involve many people in the change, to help them overcome fears, and to activate resources they may not be aware of.

The servant leadership approach developed by Robert Greenleaf shifts the leadership focus onto the interests of those being led. It expresses the inner attitude of a leader who uses his experience to support the personal development of the employees.

Greenleaf's 10 Principles of servant leadership:
1. Listening
2. Empathy
3. Healing
4. Self-awareness
5. Persuasion
6. Conceptualization
7. Foresight
8. Stewardship
9. Commitment to the growth of people
10. Building community

30 *The transformation to sustainability requires innovation at all levels of corporate management. New skills are also required, not least a tolerance for ambiguity. Dilemma management and dealing with paradoxes are just as important as the ability to deal with complexity, high dynamics and uncertainty.*

3.3 Mindfulness in the organisation

The term mindfulness has two meanings: It was and is widely used in connection with the care of the weak, sick and dying. In this context, **paying attention to the needs of other people** is called mindfulness.

The second meaning of the term comes from spirituality and characterises a special state of perception and consciousness. It is about the ability to **experience the present moment** while becoming more aware of holding one's own attention. If one extends this ability to organisations, then it is about the **ability of a system to see itself.**

Organisations in which mindfulness plays a major role are characterised by the fact that their managers lead meaningfully. There is also a clearly defined, meaningful corporate purpose. In management literature, this is currently being discussed under the heading of a **purpose-driven organisation.**

Consciously creating value based on the SDGs

The many questions and tips from the last two chapters can help companies to reflect on themselves and see clearly what they are doing. If you want to shift a company's direction towards sustainable value creation, it can make sense to use the following matrix as a communication and mapping tool.

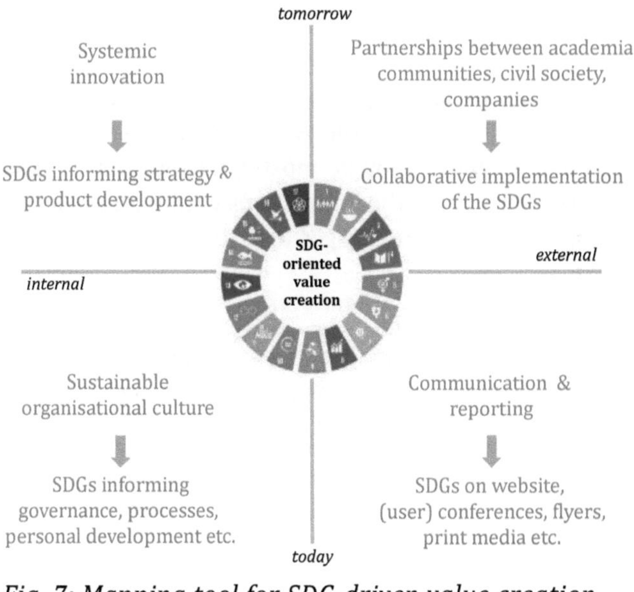

Fig. 7: Mapping tool for SDG-driven value creation

All the issues that have just been discussed can be mapped on this matrix. It can also help to map existing sustainability-related activities. Like most strategy matrices, there are two axes: A time axis forms the vertical, an organisational the horizontal. The two lower fields relate to **sustainable day-to-day operations** (Section 3.1). The two upper fields relate to **sustainable innovation** (Section 3.2).

Sustainable organisational culture

Every organisation, including every corporation, forms a culture that determines collective behaviour and the behaviour of individuals. It is the result of the interplay of values, norms, thought patterns and basic assumptions such as views of the world or people, which all employees share, though mostly unconsciously. The culture shapes both the interactions within an organisation as well as how it engages with the outside world.

What is organisational culture?
Edgar Schein, an American social scientist, defines organisational culture as follows: *'Organisational culture is a comprising number of features, including a shared pattern of basic assumptions which group members have aquired over time as they learn to successfully cope with internal and external organisationally relevant problems.'* (Schein, 1990, quoted from Wikipedia, page 'Organisational Culture')
He distinguishes between three levels:

- **Symbols and signs:** language, rituals, clothing, manners. These are visible but require interpretation.

- **Norms and standards:** maxims, 'ideologies', rules of behaviour, prohibitions. These are partly visible, partly unconscious.
- **Basic assumptions:** worldview, relation to the environment, time / truth, the essence of humans, social relationships, the essence of human relationships. These are invisible and mostly unnoticed.

Today's corporate language is usually very focused on productivity and efficiency. Many basic assumptions contradict the change in direction that is necessary to implement the SDGs. Examples are the growth myth or the success metric. **In order to direct a company to make profitable contributions to the implementation of the SDGs, it is necessary to be aware of the basic assumptions** and, if necessary, to change them – possibly in alignment with Brundtland-definition of sustainability.

Sustainability communication

The 2030 Agenda, expressed in the 17 SDGs, defines a global framework for action. At the same time, it defines a clear focus with its 169 sub-goals. Countless organisations have been working on their implementation since 2016. Corporations have been obliged to publish a **sustainability report** for a while. Many corporations use the SDGs for this reporting and many publish integrated business reports, which means that the reporting system no longer differentiates between financial and sustainability reporting, these two documents have become one. There are various internationally recognised regulations for the preparation of such reports, e.g. from the Global Reporting Initiative (GRI).

By now the **SDG symbols** can often be found in corporate communications. They form a **universal language** that helps people from all over the world and from a wide variety of fields of work to communicate quickly and intuitively on a common topic. The visual graphics are freely available and can be used by anyone, when respecting the SDG design guidelines available online.

Shaping systems transformation

Sustainable development, with respect to the Brundtland Report and the 2030 Agenda, describes a further step in the development of humanity. The aim is to create a world in which **human dignity and the well-being of planet earth** are the compass for political, social, economic and individual decision-making and action everywhere and at all times.

The great transformation
In his book *The Great Transformation*, Uwe Schneidewind from the German Wuppertal Institute presents sustainability as a cultural revolution. He classifies it as the central civilisation project of the 21st century and describes seven turning points that will have to be shaped in Germany over the next few decades: turnarounds in prosperity and consumption, in energy and resource use, in mobility and food consumption, for the urban and industrial contexts.

Systems transformation is a profound change in unconscious, established thought patterns and organisational structures. A great difficulty is to overcome the so-called **lock-in effect**. This term is mostly used in marketing to describe a close customer relationship that arises from the fact that the costs of switching to alternative products or services are very high or that other barriers make it difficult to switch to another provider. Lock-in effects can also be seen in society as a whole. The public discussion clearly shows the various **barriers to change** associated with the energy transition: wind turbines, yes, but not in my back yard. Photovoltaics on my roof, yes, but not if I can't use them myself. Offshore wind farms, yes, but no power line across my backyard. Coal exit, yes, but what about jobs? CO_2 pricing, yes, but what is the appropriate price?

We humans are creatures of habit that welcome change when we have chosen it but reject it when it is 'forced' on us. What can we do to shape the upcoming, profound changes instead of enduring them? Clarity about the desired future and trust in the possibility of mastering the transformation path together enable a profound change in attitude. Something that was initially perceived as a frightening challenge or disorder may then become an opportunity for growth and development.

Systemic innovation

Every innovation is essentially a process of **communication** and **cooperation: Which problems in which context do we solve in which way?** This is the basic question for systemic innovation. At the beginning of the process, the focus is emphatically on problem definition via a dialogue with all those affected and involved, using, among other things, consensus building for decision-making and defining the desired effects of the solution.

Problem definition

In order to define a problem in a sustainable manner, i.e. taking into account the ecological limits and social goals, it is necessary to understand and describe the problem in its context. Where did it come from? What are its facets? Which influencing factors amplify or reduce it? Which interests, needs, values play a role? What is the desired end state? Oftentimes, the real problem lies elsewhere than in the visible symptoms. It is important to include all stakeholders in defining the problem. This is a process that needs a lot of attention. Only when everyone has formed a picture of the common goal should one begin to find the solution. Taking blind action can exacerbate the problem.

Dialogue

A dialogue is a form of conversation in which the participants are keen to achieve a common understanding of the topic being discussed. The point of view of each participant is perceived as **free of prejudice** and as **equal**. This usually leads to a new and deeper understanding of the situation and builds trust between the participants. Experienced moderators or very self-reflective participants are required to support this process.

Impact orientation

In contrast to the classic innovation process, the success of a systemic innovation is not measured by the market success of a product, but by the cumulative impact of using the product. Positive effects are the benefits generated, e.g. protection against sunburn with sunscreen. Negative effects are the unwanted side effects, e.g. generation of plastic waste from the sunscreen bottle. All possible effects are identified and weighed against each other during the innovation process. The result is the most effective solution from an ecological, social, economic and customer-oriented perspective.

Consent

In situations where many parties have different needs and perspectives, there is a risk of endless circular discussions. In order to come to decisions in a reasonable timeframe, it is advisable to rely on **consent instead of consensus**. To achieve this the following rules must be observed:

- Decisions are made by one person who obtains the necessary information from all relevant parties involved.
- Justifiable and relevant objections (if possible, with better alternatives) can be introduced during the decision-making phase.
- The decision maker is responsible for implementation or delegates it after consultation with the team.

Consent decisions require the **trust of all those involved** and a **decision-maker who takes responsibility and is willing to implement.** Consent is increasingly used in agile, self-organised teams.

SDG-oriented value creation encompasses a wide range of ways in which companies can act sustainably. Profitability remains necessary. 30

Systemic innovation always begins with a problem definition in which all affected parties are included. In order to come to decisions in a reasonable timeframe, it is helpful to rely on consent instead of consensus.

The UN Sustainable Development Goals can serve as inspiration for developing a sustainable corporate culture. Sustainable development can be seen as a profound cultural revolution.

30 MINUTES

4. New knowledge, new tools

Systems transformation always builds on new knowledge, new methods and new tools. The transformation to sustainable development has been demanded for a good 30 years. Now it is finally possible and probable. In the last few decades there have been breakthroughs in knowledge in many scientific disciplines that can support this fundamental change. These have been further developed and tested in a large number of new (including social) technologies, management methods, communication and collaboration tools.

4.1 Deep data – sensible goals

At the beginning of every change there is the question: How should the future be different from today? In other words: **Where are we now and where do we want to go**? It is a question of intention, of will. But before the answer to this can be achieved the question 'Why?' needs to be asked. Because people can only change what they know.

Living means knowing

At the end of the 1960s, Humberto Maturana and Francisco Varela defined the mind or **cognition** as the actual process of life. This formed part of the framework of the **Santiago theory**, which is a **systems view of life**. According to Maturana and Varela, every living being has cognitive abilities, that is, to perceive and react to the outside world. The cognitive abilities of human beings include:

- Perception and attention,
- Memory and learning,
- Creativity, imagination, problem solving,
- Planning, orienting, structuring,
- Argumentation,
- Introspection,
- Willpower and belief.

In addition, every living being has a characterising organisational feature: **autopoiesis**. Autopoiesis refers to a living being **as a continuous process of self-cre-**

ation and self-preservation of the overall system. Previously it had been customary to define life by listing individual properties, such as mobility or irritability of cells. Autopoiesis can be used to distinguish living from non-living systems.

The mind-and-life dialogues
In 1987 Varela was the scientific coordinator and moderator of the first mind-and-life dialogue. Since then, the previously very different worlds of western scientists and spiritual leaders of eastern philosophies have been meeting every year. They exchange ideas on fundamental questions of life and consciousness.

Realising potential

New findings from brain research indicate that **our brain continues to develop throughout our lives.** Fed by joy and enthusiasm, we can learn a lot of new things in a very short time, into old age. However, if fears, resignation or competition dominate, our brain still works, but it does not develop any further. Unfortunately, there is currently a rapid increase in stress-related illnesses in the western world, which prevents those affected people from developing their potential. But there are also a steadily growing number of methods for coping with stress and dealing with one's own emotions. Various methods of personality development, self-awareness and meditation are used to increase personal **resilience** and thus well-being.

> **Holistic schooling approach**
> In 2012, German neurobiologist Gerald Hüther, together with teacher Margreth Rasfeld and legal scholar Stephan Breidenbach, founded the 'Schule im Aufbruch' (holistic schooling approach). The network advocates holistic and transformative education based on the UNESCO World Action Plan Education for Sustainable Development. It is about developing individual potential and assuming responsibility for oneself, for fellow human beings and for our planet.

Learning from the emerging future

Claus Otto Scharmer, co-founder of the Presencing Institute at Massachusetts Institute of Technology (MIT) in Cambridge, Massachusetts, distinguishes between two fundamentally different ways of learning:

- Learning by reflecting on the past and using what was successful at that time.
- Learning by sensing and **shaping emerging future possibilities.**

But how is that supposed to work? One of the great things about us humans is our imagination. It allows us to develop a picture of something that isn't there and then find ways to make that vision a reality. In other words: We can recognise (behavioural) patterns from the past, break them, and create new ones.

Recognising blind spots

In social psychology, the **blind spot refers to the parts of the self that are not noticed.** Numerous methods of personal development and spiritual practices allow the blind spots to be identified, for hidden conflicts to be resolved, and for resources that have been liberated to be used elsewhere.

Not only personalities, but also groups, organisations and societies have blind spots. These are hidden in the **social field** and are the unconscious cultural assumptions, unmentioned values and thought patterns that have arisen due to different life experiences or training. For example, physicists and sociologists have very different ideas about the use of the term 'work'.

Social field according to Scharmer
'A social or cognitive field is the expression of the quality of relationships that lead to patterns of thinking, communicating and organising, which in turn produce practical results.' (Scharmer, 2018)

Theory U: 7 types of attention

At the beginning of this millennium there was a blind spot with regards to the phenomenon 'social or cognitive field'. Today it is known that it can be recognised and changed. The U-process developed at MIT by Scharmer and his colleagues is now a well-proven method. It helps to recognise the old, no longer helpful collective behaviours and to discover and learn new behaviours, ones that are more appropriate to the goal of sustainable development. The process consists of seven steps:

1. Stop and become aware of the routines.
2. Perceive with new eyes (free of prejudice).
3. Deepen perception on feelings, thought patterns, etc.
4. **Presencing**: becoming still, feeling what is there and letting it be, letting something new come.
5. Connection of the new with your own vision and intention.
6. Creation of prototypes (a prototype helps to concretise and test the future in action).
7. Realisation by implementing the new behaviour, the different doing in the world.

Think big – act in small steps

This process can be seen as part of social innovation. It is scalable. It helps individuals and groups to visualise their own behaviour, their intention, and their goals. It enables the development of collective consciousness, the definition of meaningful, actionable goals and the change of social fields. MIT has been inviting people to participate in **Massive Open Online Courses (MOOCs)** every year since 2015, thus forming a rapidly growing network of change agents. Smart use of digital technologies makes this possible.

Life never changes in isolation, but always in interaction, i.e. through learning together within one's context. Lifelong learning is nourished by joy and enthusiasm. The U-process describes a method by which one can learn from the emerging future. This is necessary in order to shape systems change. 30

4.2 Big data – informed decisions

There is a new buzz word that has been used in the public media for several years: Big Data. What is it all about? Where does all the new data come from? Can they be useful for us to shape the transformation towards sustainability?

Big Data

Big data is about **large, complex, rapidly changing amounts of data**. They are usually too weakly structured to be evaluated using conventional data processing methods. The same term is increasingly used for the technologies that are used to evaluate big data. The 'big' refers to the six 'V-dimensions':

- **Volume** (size, data volume),
- **Velocity** (speed at which the data volumes are generated and transferred),
- **Variety** (different data types and sources),
- **Veracity** (authenticity of data),

- **Value** (commercial added value),
- **Validity** (ensuring high data quality).

Big data is created through the use of **social media**, but also through the **increasing number of sensors** that are, for example, used in smart houses and cities. The Internet of Things (IoT) is the basis for smart innovations and an enormous data source.

Sensors

'Only what gets measured gets done' is common business wisdom. But how do you measure systemic developments such as the recovery of nature or changes in the behaviour of societies? In the last few decades, a large number of different sensors have become very **energy-efficient** and **inexpensive**. They can be used to measure and observe chemical, physical, ecological and many other properties. This can be very useful, for example, for the observation and regeneration of endangered ecosystems.

Internet of Things & robots

The Internet of Things is the collective term for technologies that **enable physical and virtual objects to be connected with one another**, and that allow them to work together via information and communication technologies. It has been created since the beginning of the millennium and in the long term will be an important building block for the realisation of the circular economy. For example, it opens up the possibility of tracking the location and condition of physical objects. In future, it will enable the control and maintenance of devices over great distances. Robotics has also developed rapidly over the past few decades. In the future, robots can provide low risk access to places that are dangerous or inaccessible to humans. This can be very helpful for the maintenance of offshore wind farms or solar systems in the desert, for example.

Analytics

Analytics or analytical information systems are processes that analyse and process all of a company's data in such a way that they support **decision-making**. In 2012, the Gartner market research group distinguished four types of analytics:

1. Descriptive analytics

What happened? Descriptive analysis looks at data from the past and seeks to understand effects on the present. It corresponds to the forecasting approach from Section 2.3. Actual data in spreadsheets, descriptive statistics and dashboards are typical examples of how this data is collected and represented. Business intelligence also fits in here.

2. Diagnostic analytics

Why did something happen? Diagnostic analytics provides answers to questions about the reasons, effects, interactions or consequences of events.

3. Predictive analytics

What will happen? Predictive analytics looks to the future. Data that is collected via sensors, websites or other technology sources is analysed for patterns and anomalies using machine learning and other statistical methods in order to make predictions about the probability of future events. Predictive maintenance is a well-known example: Anomalies in sensor data of a machine predict the failure of certain components and initiate maintenance.

4. Prescriptive analytics

How do we have to act so that a future event does (does not) occur? Prescriptive analytics provides recommendations for action in order to influence trends in a desired direction, prevent forecast developments or prepare for a future event. Sophisticated mathematical models based on expert knowledge, which are developed under the term 'Operations Research', are the basis of this. **Artificial intelligence** and **machine learning** are also used here.

Prescriptive analytics can **support the backcasting processes.** It is therefore particularly suitable for complex strategic decisions which will be increasingly required of organisations as a result of sustainable development.

Interaction between man and machine

Will computers replace human thinking, just as machines have replaced our physical abilities since the beginning of industrialisation? No! However, digital technologies can relieve us of routine tasks which allows more time to deal with exceptional situations in a sensible and measured manner. By choosing to use smart algorithms, decision-makers can achieve a new quality of efficiency, process stability and resilience.

> **Agile optimisation**
> Adrian Weiler, Eva Savelsberg and Ulrich Dorndorf describe a new management approach in their book 'Agile Optimierung' (only available in German). It allows executives to make complex decisions with the help of data and to master the seemingly unpredictable in a resource-efficient manner.

The rapid development and spread of digital technologies enable us today to observe and control 30
highly complex dynamic processes. Prescriptive analytics supports decision-making in unpredictable situations, and a change of course towards a desired future.

4.3 The twin path

Systems thinking and acting assumes that everything is connected to everything and that nothing exists in isolation from its environment. It differs fundamentally from the way in which we have organised ourselves in the last few centuries, with the division of labour, the creation of expert silos, different industries, and social groups.

Thinking models of sustainability

From as early as 1992, at the first global UN sustainability conference in Rio, the **triple bottom line** represented by three '**overlapping circles**' was presented to visualise the systemic approach to sustainability. The three 'Ps' - planet (ecology), people (social), profit (economy) - are seen as equal and equally important. Sustainable development exists where the three areas overlap (see Figure 8 first graph).

The sustainability '**model of nested circles**' was introduced just ten years later. It illustrates another relationship between the three 'Ps': no economy without society; no society without ecology (see Figure 8 second graph).

If we want to shape the transformation towards sustainability, both models have a weak point. They represent relationships at a macro level, between large systems. However, development and change take place at a micro level, in the interaction between the individual and the environment. Therefore, a **fourth 'P'** was added to the 2011 priority model: the **person** (see figure 8 third graph).

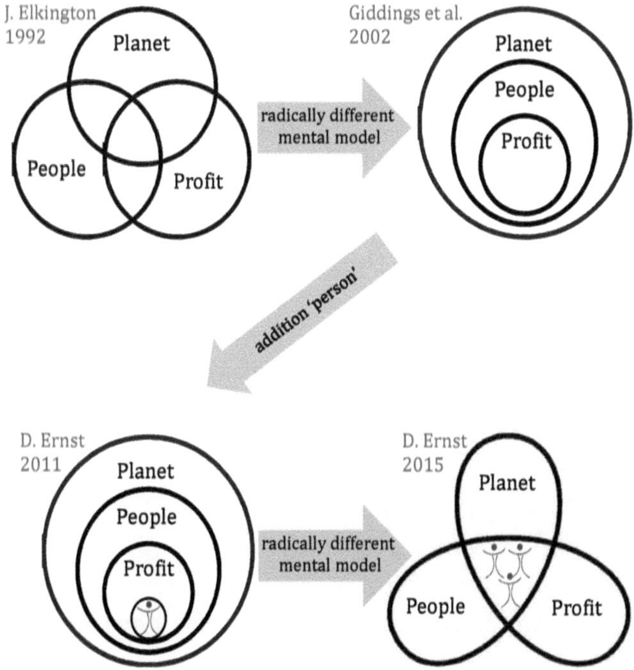

Fig. 8: Evolution of mental models for sustainability driven economy and business

None of these models take into account the fact that everything is connected to everything. However, this is expressed in the fourth model, which I call the **balance-trilog**. It uses the Trinity symbol as its basic structure. **Sustainability is achieved when all four fields are of the same size, that is, when they are in balance** (see figure 8 last graph).

Levers for re-balancing

There is probably a relatively high degree of agreement in the world that many of our ecological and social systems have become unbalanced in favour of the economy. In addition, the number of people who suffer from burnout, stress and overwork, partly due to working conditions, has increased rapidly in recent years. This can be represented through the imbalance of the trilog.

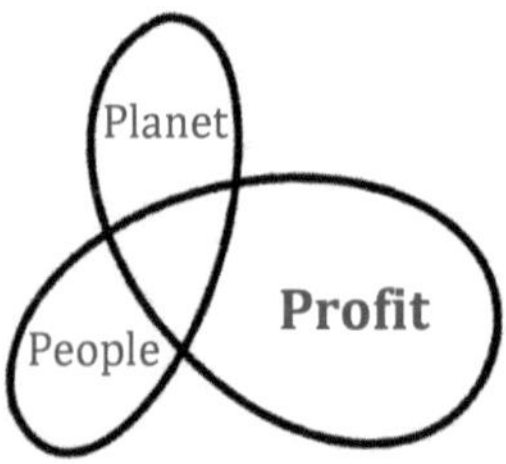

Fig. 9: Not sustainable situation today: dominance of profit over planet and people

How do we get back into balance? I believe that an **important lever is available to each of us.** If we personally manage to consciously lead a sustainable, healthy, balanced life, we also learn to intuitively feel the levers that lead to the rebalancing of our environment. Why? Life often works on the principle of **self-similarity**, which Aristotle expressed as follows: 'Know yourself, then you will know the world.'

Self-similarity
Self-similarity describes recurring structures that are nested in themselves. The term is used in philosophy and sociology as well as in the natural sciences and mathematics. Examples are blood vessels, fern leaves or cauliflower florets where the whole is exactly or approximately similar to one of its parts.

The following assumptions and observations have helped me to find this lever:

- Humanity and its development are part of a great systemic evolutionary process.
- The distinction between body, mind and soul is useful in order to grasp very different aspects of human life.
- Basically, every person has the ability to develop self-awareness. This includes the ability to witness your own feelings, thoughts, body signals and movements.

René Descartes postulated 'Cogito, ergo sum' ('I think, therefore I am'). That is, he defines humans as their minds. This idea has shaped our western image of people for a long time. But today there is scientific evidence: **body, mind and soul are inextricably linked**.

If we now use the principle of self-similarity, we may conclude:

- Ecology can be assigned to the body.
- Social issues correspond to the soul.
- Economy can be associated with the mind.

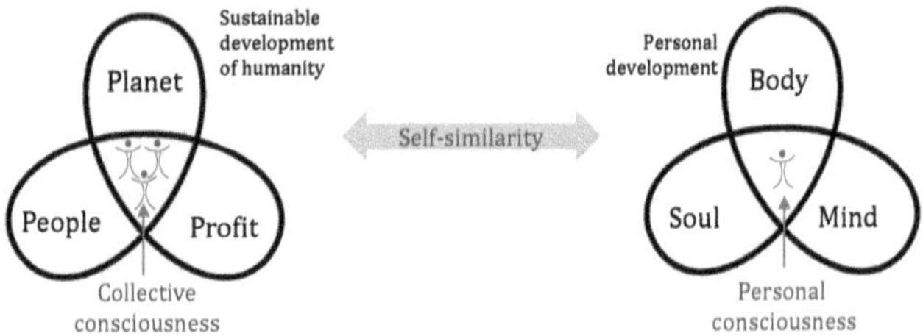

Fig. 10: Self-similarity applied to the balance-trilog

The path to sustainability requires a profound shift of both our individual and collective consciousness. This happens when many people begin to tell new stories and narratives. Different decisions and changed behaviours will then follow from these new stories.

It is known that no one has the capacity to change others. You can only change and develop yourself. Everyone can choose a sustainability-oriented lifestyle at the personal level. The pathway to personal balance is the development of deep self-awareness and self-management. This is an **inner path** of consciousness development that will lead to different decisions and activities in the world.

Native Americans call one such path the **twin path of leadership:**
'We do not trust any leader who does not follow the twin trail – the inner trail of self-understanding, self-unfolding and deepening; the outer trail of action and powerful

effect in the world. The outer trail of having effect in the world is hugely important, but without the ongoing wisdom trail of the inner path, it will inevitably become hostile to the greater good.' (Foreword of Mac McCartney in Ernst, 2016)

30

Systemic thinking and acting are important keys to implementing the UN Sustainable Development Goals. This is expressed in the 'balance-trilog' from the areas of planet, people and profit. A worthwhile way to learn systems thinking and acting is to develop self-understanding and learn to lead yourself. The twin path describes an old tradition of leadership: the inner path of self-understanding paired with the outer path of effect in the world. The transformation to sustainable development can be carried out by walking the twin path.

Nine do's from lived practice

1. Create awareness

Amazingly, the UN Sustainable Development Goals are still a well-kept secret – even though they form the only stable long-term framework for politics and business. Make your employees and colleagues aware of the goals and point out the necessary changes and possible opportunities associated with them.

2. Expect a long journey

The transformation to sustainable development requires all stakeholder groups to work together, sometimes in a new way. This is necessary in order to shape the upcoming systems changes. These are linked to changes in unconscious cultural behaviours and beliefs. Processes of creating awareness and learning new behaviour are inherently lengthy and require patience and perseverance.

3. Start

There's no one right place, no one right activity to start. Possible starting points are as diverse as the people who find them. Someone accompanies their children on a Friday-for-Future demonstration, someone else is involved in voluntary work. A third party uses their professional position to check innovations for sustainable effects. Wherever you are, the first step is usually the hardest. Still, start looking at what you can do to contribute.

4. Be mindful of language

Conflicts often arise because the creators and those affected by a transformation have different levels of experience and thought structures. It is therefore imperative to be very conscious of language right from the start by:

- Avoiding technical language, use everyday language,
- Shaping dialogue, use positive, inclusive language,
- Using metaphors and visualisations,
- Providing regular feedback,
- Highlighting the variety of perspectives.

5. Develop yourself

Make it clear that no one is to blame for the current situation. We have all gotten entangled in thinking models and evaluation mechanisms that are no longer effective. It is now our task to become aware of the resulting blind spots. We can then free ourselves from the entanglement and look openly and boldly into a life-enhancing future.

6. Formulate a meaningful goal

In order to shape the future together, it is essential to define a common goal. This vision expresses the wishes and needs of everyone involved. The goal should be clear and easy to understand. The vision should not describe the way to achieve the goal!

7. Courage and confidence

It takes courage to break new ground. Put trust in people who develop this courage. Help them if something doesn't work out. Perhaps then you too will develop the courage to change.

8. Be mindful of time

Time is a gift of life to us. How do we deal with it? Do we use it consciously, do we let ourselves drift or do we just function? Create a good balance between the three time dimensions:

- **Kairos,** the right moment, one you can only recognise when there is some space and stillness,
- **Chronos**, scheduled time that we so easily use and overload,
- **Rhythm**, the rhythms that every life follows.

9. Never give up!

Believe that everything will be well in the end. There is always a way!

Fast Reader

1. The state of the world

Life expectancy, standard of living, general level of education and much more have improved impressively since the late 18th century. However, mankind's progress has a price that is becoming visible today. Countries that do well in the social dimension of sustainability – such as Germany, for example – leave a particularly large ecological footprint.

We live in times of double systems transformation:

- ***Digitisation brings about major changes in the way we communicate and deal with data and information. We all learn new cultural skills.***
- ***At the same time – coupled with the term sustainability – the transformation of our global economic system is taking place. In the future, economic success will no longer be measured only in terms of profitability, but also in the creation of social and ecological benefits.***

2. Sustainable development

The 17 UN Sustainable Development Goals, jointly defined by the 193 states represented at the UN, form the agenda for the peaceful and sustainable development of humanity. Sub-goals have been defined for each of these goals. There are 169 in total. They are to be achieved by 2030.

No stakeholder group nor nation alone can implement them on its own. Therefore, everyone is called to contribute. In most countries around the world, work has been going on since 2016 to translate the goals and sub-goals into concrete measures. This is a very creative process because all measures need to make sense in their geographical and cultural context.

30 ***Since the implementation of the UN Sustainable Development Goals can be understood as an intermediate step in the profound transformation of our global economic system, backcasting is an ideal planning method:***

- ***First, the problem is defined.***
- ***Then all those affected formulate a vision together.***
- ***The actual situation is determined.***
- ***Ideas to achieve the vision are generated.***

- ***The ideas are prioritised.***
- ***The implementation of the ideas is agile.***

3. Sustainable business

There are many ways to make day-to-day business in a company more sustainable: sustainable supply chains, green IT, feedback culture, etc. However, when it comes to implementation, conflicting goals and dilemmas are probable to arise. The transformation to sustainability therefore also requires innovation at all levels. People who want to shape this need to be tolerant of ambiguity. They have to be able to deal with contradictions, as well as with complexity, high dynamics and uncertainty.

Companies have a wide range of options for acting sustainably. The following applies: 30

- ***Profitability is a necessary boundary condition.***
- ***The UN Sustainable Development Goals can serve as inspiration for developing a sustainable corporate culture.***
- ***Systemic innovation always begins with problem definition in which all those affected are included.***
- ***In order to come to decisions quickly, it is helpful to rely on consent instead of consensus.***

- ***Sustainable development can be seen as a profound cultural revolution.***

4. New knowledge, new tools

Life never changes in isolation, but always in interaction, that is, in joint learning with one's context. Lifelong learning is nourished by joy and enthusiasm. It is necessary to shape systems transformation.

The development and spread of digital technologies enable us to observe and control highly complex, dynamic processes. Prescriptive analytics supports decision-making in unpredictable situations and a change of direction towards a desired future.

Systematic thinking and acting are important keys to implementing the UN Sustainable Development Goals. A worthwhile way to do this is to develop self-awareness and learn to lead oneself.

The transformation to sustainable development can be well shaped while walking the twin path of leadership:

- ***the inner path of self-understanding, self-unfolding and deepening coupled with***
- ***the outer path of action and powerful effect in the world.***

About the author

Dr. Dorothea Ernst works with executives and teams, accompanies personal and organisational transformation processes. She is sustainability catalyst at INFORM in Aachen, Germany. She holds a PhD of physics and is a mediator, author and public speaker. For 16 years she has worked at Philips, helping to shape innovation and change processes. Two important stages were the collaboration in the digitisation of the lighting industry, and the introduction of sustainability as an innovative force for the whole of Philips. In both assignments she learned that people and their goals, values and attitudes in combination with smart use of technology are the essential ingredients for innovation and long-term, life-affirming success.

Contact:
Dr. Dorothea Ernst
D.Ernst@celviva.com

Further reading

- Capra, F., Luisi, P.L.: The Systems View of Life, Cambridge University Press, Cambridge, 2015
- Ernst, D.: Personal and Organizational Transformation towards Sustainability, Business Expert Press, New York, 2016
- Felber, C.: Change Everything: Creating an Economy for the Common Good , Zed Books, London, 2015
- Hüther, G.: Was wir sind und was wir sein könnten, Fischer Verlag, Frankfurt, 2011
- KPMG: A New Vision of Value, https://assets.kpmg/content/dam/kpmg/pdf/2014/10/a-new-vision-of-value-v1.pdf [27.09.2021]
- Maturana, H.R., Varela, F.J.: Der Baum der Erkenntnis, Scherz Verlag, Bern, München, Wien, 1987
- Meadows, D. et al.: The Limits to Growth: A Report to the Club of Rome, Universe Books, New York, 1972
- PwC: Measuring and managing total impact: A new language for business decisions, https://www.pwc.com/gx/en/sustainability/publications/total-im-

pact-measurement-management/assets/pwc-timm-report.pdf [27.09.2021]

- Rockström, J., Steffen, W., Noone, K. et al.: A safe operating space for humanity. Nature 461, 472–475, 2009

- Scharmer, C.O.: The Essentials of Theory U: Core Principles and Applications, Berrett-Koehler Publishers, Oakland, 2018

- Schein, E.H.: Organizational Culture and Leadership, 5th edition, Wiley, 2016

- Schneidewind, U.: Die große Transformation, Fischer Verlag, Frankfurt, 2018

- Senge, P.: The fifth Discipline: The Art & Practice of the Learning Organisation, 2nd edition, Currency, 2006

- The Natural Step Deutschland. HDI – Human Development Index, https://www.thenaturalstep.de/de/situation/human-development-index/ [27.09.2021]

- TWI2050: The World in 2050 – Annual Report 2017, https://www.iiasa.ac.at/web/home/research/twi/Annual_Report_TWI2050.pdf [27.09.2019]

- United Nations: Transforming our World – The Agenda 2030 for Sustainable Development, https://sustainabledevelopment.un.org/post2015/transformingourworld/publication [27.09.2021]

- Weiler, A., Savelsberg, E., Dorndorf, U.: Agile Optimierung in Unternehmen, Haufe, Freiburg, 2018

- Wissenschaftlicher Beirat der Bundesregierung Globale Umweltveränderungen: Our Common Digital Future, WBGU, Berlin, 2019

- World Commission on the Environment and Development: Our Common Future, Oxford University Press, Oxford, 1987

- WWF, Living Planet Report 2006, https://d2ouvy59p0dg6k.cloudfront.net/downloads/living_planet_report.pdf, p. 19 [27.09.2021]

Index